Who is Allâh and His Prophet ﷺ

First Edition: December 2001

Supervised by:
ABDUL MALIK MUJAHID

K.S.A.
- **Riyadh**
  Darussalam Showroom:
  Tel 00966-1-4614483 Fax: 4644945
- **Jeddah**
  Darussalam Showroom:
  Tel: 00966-2-6879254
- Fax: 00966-2-6336270
  Al-Khobar
  Darussalam Showroom:
  Tel: 00966-3-8692900
  Fax: 00966-3-8691551

U.A.E
- Darussalam, Sharjah U.A.E
  Tel: 00971-6-5632623 Fax: 5632624

Pakistan
- Darussalam, 50 Lower Mall, Lahore
  Tel: 0092-42-724 0024 Fax: 7354072
  Rahman Market, Ghazni Street
- Urdu Bazar Lahore
  Tel: 0092-42-7120054 Fax: 7320703

U.S.A
- Darussalam, Houston
  P.O Box: 79194 Tx 772779
  Tel: 001-713-722 0419
  Fax: 001-713-722 0431
  E-mail: sales@dar-us-salam.com
- Darussalam, New York
  572 Atlantic Ave, Brooklyn
  New York-11217, Tel: 001-718-625 5925

U.K
- Darussalam International Publications Ltd.
  226 High Street, Walthamstow,
  London E17 7JH, Tel: 0044-208 520 2666
  Mobile: 0044-794 730 6706
  Fax: 0044-208 521 7645
- Darussalam International Publications Limited
  Regent Park Mosque, 146 Park Road,
  London Nw8 7RG Tel: 0044-207 724 3363

France
- Editions & Librairie Essalam
  135, Bd de Ménilmontant- 75011 Paris
  Tél: 0033-01- 43 38 19 56/ 44 83
  Fax: 0033-01- 43 57 44 31
  E-mail: essalam@essalam.com

Australia
- ICIS: Ground Floor 165-171, Haldon St.
  Lakemba NSW 2195, Australia
  Tel: 00612 9758 4040 Fax: 9758 4030

Malaysia
- E&D Books SDN. BHD.-321 B 3rd Floor,
  Suria Klcc
  Kuala Lumpur City Center 50088
  Tel: 00603-21663433 Fax: 459 72032

Singapore
- Muslim Converts Association of Singapore
  32 Onan Road The Galaxy
  Singapore- 424484
  Tel: 0065-440 6924, 348 8344
  Fax: 440 6724

Sri Lanka
- Darul Kitab 6, Nirmal Road, Colombo-4
  Tel: 0094-1-589 038 Fax: 0094-74 722433

Kuwait
- Islam Presentation Committee
  Enlightment Book Shop
  P.O. Box: 1613, Safat 13017 Kuwait
  Tel: 00965-244 7526, Fax: 240 0057

India
- Islamic Dimensions
  56/58 Tandel Street (North)
  Dongri, Mumbai 4000 009,India
  Tel: 0091-22-3736875, Fax: 3730689
  E-mail:sales@IRF.net

South Africa
- Islamic Da`wah Movement (IDM)
  48009 Qualbert 4078 Durban,South Africa
  Tel: 0027-31-304-6883
  Fax: 0027-31-305-1292
  E-mail: idm@ion.co.za

Who is Allâh and His Prophet ﷺ

Compiled by
Research Division Darussalam

DARUSSALAM
GLOBAL LEADER IN ISLAMIC BOOKS
Riyadh · Jeddah · Sharjah · Lahore
London · Houston · New York

Publishers Note

Who is Allâh and His Prophet is part of 'For the Seeker of Truth' series. For any seeker of truth, anywhere, it is incumbent to know where we came from and where we are going. Does the truth exist? In what form does it exist? How does it exist? The beginning of everything is with the Creator, Allâh. The created being that knew him best was Muhammad ﷺ.This booklet we hope, *Inshâ' Allah*, will serve as a short introduction on this most serious of subjects.

We, at Darussalam, designed this series for new Muslims and Non-Muslims to try and give them a balanced overview of a very vast subject. When you begin the study of a huge body of material, it is important to understand the basics or fundamentals of your subject. It will always serve you well in your later studies. In His book, the Noble Qur'ân Allâh has instructed all of us many times to seek knowledge. He mentions references to people of knowledge and understanding. In this day and age, it seems more important to know what a man has rather than who he is. It seems like it is more important to be known as being smart than to be known as truthful. When one is respected more for knowing how to use someone else rather than understand him, in these times, we at Darussalam would like to support, in every way possible, those who consider themselves as Seekers of the Truth.

Abdul Malik Mujahid
General Manager
Darussalam

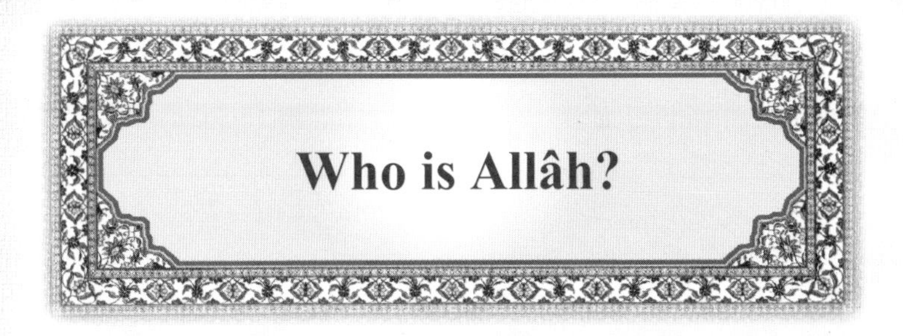

Who is Allâh?

Allâh is the proper name applied to the One True Divine God Who exists necessarily by Himself, Whose most beautiful Names describe His Divine Attributes. Allâh says:

> "He is Allâh, beside Whom *Lâ ilâha illa Huwa* (none has the right to be worshipped but He), the King, the Holy, the One Free from all defects, the Giver of security, the Watcher over His creatures, the All-Mighty, the Compeller, the Supreme. Glorified is Allâh! (High is He) above all that they associate as partners with Him. He is Allâh, the Creator, the Inventor of all things, the Bestower of forms. To Him belong the best names. All that is in the heavens and the earth glorify Him. And He is the All-Mighty, the All-Wise." (*Sûrat Al-Hashr,* 59: 23,24)

Allâh is the One, the Sole, the Indivisible and Unique. He has neither a son nor a partner nor an equal. He is the Sole Creator and Sustainer of the universe. His Essence does not resemble any essence. He is not contained in anything, nor is anything contained in Him. "There is none like unto Him." Allâh says:

> "Say (O Muhammad ﷺ): 'He is Allâh, (the) One. *Allâh-us-Samad* [Allâh the Self-Sufficient Master, Whom all creatures need, (He neither eats nor drinks)].

He begets not, nor was He begotten. And there is none coequal or comparable unto Him." (*Sûrat Al-Ikhlâs,* 112:1-4)

He is the Creator in Whose Hand is the disposal of all affairs, Allâh is the Omnipotent and the Omniscient. Allâh says:

"The Originator of the heavens and the earth. When He decrees a matter, He only says to it : Be!– and it is." (*Sûrat Al-Baqarah,* 2:117)

There is none to resist His Command, or alter His Decision. He is the Merciful Whose Mercy encompasses everything. The Prophet Mûsâ عليه السلام describes Allâh:

"You are the Most Merciful of those who show mercy." (*Sûrat Al-A'râf,* 7:151)

Allâh says:

"My Mercy embraces all things." (*Sûrat Al-A'râf,* 7:156)

He is Wise in all His Actions and Just in all His Decrees. His Justice ensures order in the universe in which nothing is out of order. Allâh says:

"Allâh bears witness that *Lâ ilâha illa Huwa* (none has the right to be worshipped but He), and the angels, and those having knowledge (also give this witness); (He always) maintains His creation in justice. *Lâ ilâha illa Huwa* (none has the right to be worshipped but He), the All-Mighty, the All-Wise." (*Sûrat Al-'Imrân,* 3:18)

There is no one to share His domain nor does He need an aide or supporter, let alone taking a son.

He is above the seven heavens, above His Throne, raising Himself in a manner that suits His Grandeur and Majesty.

Allâh says:

"Indeed, your Lord is Allâh, Who created the heavens and the earth in Six Days, and then He rose over *(Istawâ)* the Throne (really in a manner that suits His Majesty). He brings the night as a cover over the day, seeking it rapidly, and (He created) the sun, the moon, the stars subjected to His Command. Surely, His is the creation and commandment. Blessed is Allâh, the Lord

of the '*Alamîn* (mankind, jinn and all that exists)!" (*Sûrat Al-A'râf,* 7:54)

"And He is Oft-Forgiving, full of love (towards the pious who are real true believers of Islamic Monotheism), Owner of the Throne, the Glorious, (He is the) Doer of whatsoever He intends (or wills)"

(*Sûrat Al-Burûj,* 85:14-16)

Allâh has revealed His Final Scripture, the Qur'ân, to the last of His Messengers, Muhammad ﷺ who was responsible for conveying the Message of Islam to mankind. Allâh says:

"Say (O Muhammad ﷺ): O mankind! Verily, I am sent to you all as the Messenger of Allâh – to Whom belongs the dominion of the heavens and the earth. *Lâ ilâha illa Huwa* (none has the right to be worshipped but He). It is He Who gives life and causes death. So believe in Allâh and His Messenger (Muhammad ﷺ), the Prophet who can neither read nor write (i.e. Muhammad ﷺ), who believes in Allâh and His Words [(this Qur'ân), the Taurât (Torâh) and the Injeel (Gospel) and also Allâh's Word: "Be!" – and he was, i.e. 'Isâ (Jesus) son of Maryam (Mary), عليهما السلام], and follow him so that you may be guided." (*Sûrat Al-A'râf,* 7:158)

He is the Exalted Allâh. Glory be to Him. He is far removed from every imperfection. Allâh says:

"*Allâh! Lâ ilâha illa Huwa* (none has the right to be worshipped but He), *Al-Hayyul-Qayyum* (the Ever

Living, the One Who sustains and protects all that exists). Neither slumber nor sleep overtakes Him. To Him belongs whatever is in the heavens and whatever is on the earth. Who is he that can intercede with Him except with His Permission? He knows what happens to them (His creatures) in this world, and what will happen to them in the Hereafter. And they will never encompass anything of His Knowledge except that which He wills. His *Kursî* extends over the heavens and the earth, and He feels no fatigue in guarding and preserving them. And He is the Most High, the Most Great." (*Sûrat Al-Baqarah,* 2:255)

Allâh is the Lord, the Creator, the Sovereign and the Manager of all affairs. He is the true God and all the other deities are false. He has no associate in His Divinity, His Lordship, His Godship, His Names or His Attributes, Allâh says:

"Lord of the heavens and the earth, and all that is between them, so worship Him (Alone) and be constant and patient in His worship. Do you know of any who is similar to Him? (of course, none is similar or co-equal or comparable to Him, and He has none as partner with Him). [There is nothing like Him and He is the All-Hearer, the All-Seer]. (*Sûrat Maryam,* 19:65)

Allâh is Ever Lasting, Self-Subsisting, the Sustainer. He is the Omniscient, Whose knowledge comprehends in the most

perfect manner all things, hidden or open, the small and the great:

> "And whether you keep your talk secret or disclose it, verily, He is the All-Knower of what is in the breasts (of men). Should not He Who has created know? And He is the Most Kind and Courteous, All-Aware (of everything)." (*Sûrat Al-Mulk,* 67:13-14)

> "Nothing is absent from His Knowledge, nor anything is hidden from Him even if it be the weight of the smallest ant" (*Sûrat Yunus,* 10:61). "Whether at rest or in motion, the state of things is known to Him prior to and during its occurrence. He neither is unaware nor forgets." (*Sûrat Tâ-Hâ,* 20:52)

Allâh is the Compassionate, the Merciful Whose mercy encompasses all things. He is far removed from injustice or tyranny.

> "And not one will your Lord treat with injustice." (*Sûrat Al-Kahf,* 18:49)

> "Verily Allâh wrongs not mankind in aught, but mankind wrong themselves." (*Sûrat Yûnus,* 10:44)

There is nothing to frustrate His Power or ability to accomplish anything; if He wants something, He simply says "Be!" and it is:

> "Nor is Allâh to be frustrated by anything whatever in the heavens or on earth: for Allâh is All-Knowing, All-

Powerful." (*Sûrat Fâtir,* 35:44)

The preservation of the heavens and the earth does by no means burden Him:

> “His Kursi does extend over the heavens and the earth, and He feels no fatigue in guarding and preserving them. And He is the Most High, the Most Great.” (*Sûrat Al-Baqarah,* 2:255)

He is the Living and the Ever Lasting, Neither slumber nor sleep seize Him. To Him belongs the kingdom of the heavens and the earth:

> "He creates what He pleases. He gives, to whom He wills, females; and He gives, to whom He wills, males, or He couples them, males and females; and He makes whom He wills barren. Surely, He is the Knowing, the Powerful." (*Sûrat Ash-Shûra,* 42:49-50)

He is the Knower of the seen and the unseen.

There is no creature that moves in the earth but its provision depends on Allâh. He knows its dwelling and its resting place:

> "He alone has the knowledge of the Hour, sends down rain and knows what is in the wombs. No soul knows what it shall earn tomorrow, and no soul knows in which land it shall die. Surely, Allâh is All-Knowing, All-A ware." (*Sûrat Luqmân,* 31:34)

His Words are the most truthful in conveying information, the most just in ruling, and the fairest in conversation:

"The Word of your Lord has been fulfilled in truth and justice." (*Sûrat Al-An'âm,* 6:115)

He is well above His creatures in His Self and His Attributes because He says about Himself:

"He is the High, the Great." (*Sûrat Al-Baqarah,* 2:220)

"He is supreme over His servants, and He is the Wise, the All-Aware." (*Sûrat Al-An`âm,* 6:18)

His Signs are everywhere and He draws our attention in many Verses of the Qur'ân to contemplate them and realize His Lordship, and thus turn to Him and worship Him:

"And among His Signs is this that He created you (Adam) from dust, and then [Hawwâ' (Eve) from Adam's rib, and then his offspring from semen, and]– behold, you are human beings scattered! And among His Signs is this that He created for you wives from among yourselves, that you may find repose in them, and He has put between you affection and mercy. Verily, in that are indeed signs for a people who reflect. And among His Signs is the creation of the heavens and the earth, and the difference of your languages and colours. Verily, in that are indeed signs for men of sound knowledge. And among His Signs is your sleep by night and by day, and your seeking of His Bounty.

Verily in that are indeed signs for a people who listen. And among His Signs is that He shows you the lightning, for fear and for hope, and He sends down water (rain) from the sky, and therewith revives the earth after its death. Verily, in that are indeed signs for a people who understand. And among His Signs is that the heaven and the earth stand by His Command. Then afterwards when He will call you by a single call, behold, you will come out from the earth (i.e., from your graves for reckoning and recompense). To Him belongs whatever is in the heavens and the earth. All are obedient to Him." (*Sûrat Ar-Rûm,* 30:20-26)

"He has created the heavens without any pillars that you see, and has set on the earth firm mountains lest it should shake with you. And He has scattered therein moving (living) creatures of all kinds. And We send down water (rain) from the sky, and We cause (plants) of every goodly kind to grow therein. This is the creation of Allâh. So, show Me that which those (whom you worship) besides Him have created. Nay,

the *Zâlimûn* (polytheists, wrongdoers and those who do not believe in the Oneness of Allâh) are in plain error." (*Sûrat Luqmân,* 31:10-11)

"Verily, it is Allâh Who causes the seed grain and the fruit stone (like date stone) to split and sprout. He brings forth the living from the dead, and it is He Who

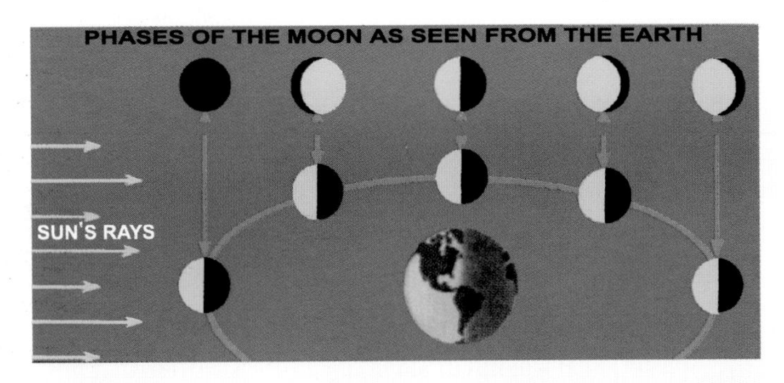

brings forth the dead from the living. Such is Allâh, then how are you deluded way from the truth? (He is the) Cleaver of the daybreak. He has appointed the night for resting, and the sun and the moon for reckoning. Such is the measuring of the All-Mighty, the All-Knowing. It is He Who has set the stars for you, so that you may guide your course with their help through the darkness of the land and the sea. We have (indeed) explained in detail Our *Ayât* (proofs, evidences, verses, lessons, signs, revelations, etc.) for people who know. It is He Who has created you from a single person (Adam), and has given you a place of residing (on the earth or in your mother's wombs) and a place of storage

[in the earth (in your graves) or in your father's loins]. Indeed, We have explained in detail Our Revelations (this Qur'ân) for people who understand. It is He Who sends down water (rain) from the sky, and with it We bring forth vegetation of all kinds, and out of it We bring forth green stalks, from which We bring forth thick clustered grain. And out of the date palm and its spathe come forth clusters of dates hanging low and near, and gardens of grapes, olives and pomegranates, each similar (in kind) yet different (in variety) and taste). Look at their fruits when they begin to bear, and the ripeness thereof. Verily, in these things there are signs for people who believe." (*Sûrat Al-An'âm,* 6:95-99)

He has no equal because His Attributes are perfect. He does not do injustice to anybody because His fairness is perfect.

He is All Aware of all His servants' deeds because of His perfect supervision and comprehensive knowledge. Our most hidden motives are known to Him at all times:

"He knows what is manifest and what is hidden."

(*Sûrat Al-A`lâ,* 87:7)

"Neither you (O Muhammad ﷺ) do any deed nor recite any portion of the Qur'ân, – nor you (O mankind) do any deed (good or evil), but We are Witness thereof when you are doing it. And nothing is hidden from your Lord (so much as) the weight of an atom (or small ant) on the earth or in the heaven. Not what is less than that or what is greater than that but is (written) in a Clear Record." (*Sûrat Yûnus,* 10:61)

"And with Him are the keys of the *Ghaib* (all that is hidden), none knows them but He. And He knows whatever there is in the land and in the sea; not a leaf falls, but He knows it. There is not a grain in the darkness of the earth nor anything fresh or dry, but is written in a Clear Record." (*Sûrat Al-An`âm,* 6:59)

"Allâh knows what every female bears, and by how much the wombs fall short (of their time or number) or exceed. Everything with Him is in (due) proportion. All-Knower of the unseen and the seen, the most Great, the Most High. It is the same (to Him) whether any of you conceals his speech or declares it openly, whether he be hid by night or goes forth freely by day." (*Sûrat Ar-Ra`d,* 13:8-10)

The Source of the Divine Messages

There is one source of all the Divine Scriptures. Allâh says:

> "It is He Who has sent down the Book (the Qur'ân) to you (Muhammad ﷺ) with truth, confirming what came before it. And He sent down the *Taurât* (Torah) and the *Injîl* (Gospel). Aforetime, as a guidance to mankind. And He sent down the Criterion [of judgement between right and wrong (this Qur'ân)]. Truly, those who disbelieve in the *Âyât* (proofs, evidences, verses, lessons, signs, revelations, etc.) of Allâh, for them there is a severe torment; and Allâh is All-Mighty, All-Able of Retribution." (*Sûrat Al-'Imrân,* 3:3-4)

Allâh revealed them for one single purpose that is, to guide mankind to the Straight Path which leads them to prosperity in this world and in the world to come, by professing His Oneness and dedicating their acts of worship exclusively to Him. Allâh says:

> "Verily, this Qur'ân guides to that which is most just and right and gives glad tidings to the believers (in the Oneness of Allâh and His Messenger Muhammad ﷺ), who work deeds of righteousness, that they shall have a great reward (Paradise)." (*Sûrat Al-Isrâ'*, 17:9)

"The month of Ramadan in which was revealed the Qur'ân, a guidance for mankind and clear proofs for the guidance and the criterion (between right and wrong)." (*Sûrat Al-Baqarah,* 2:185)

Each of the previous Messengers was sent to his own people, but Muhammad ﷺ was sent to mankind at large.

What is the Qur'ân?

The Qur'ân is Allâh's Word, not a created thing, nor is it an attribute of any created thing. Jibreel (Gabriel) brought down the Qur'ân to Muhammad ﷺ in stages as circumstances warranted over a period of twenty-three years. Allâh says:

"And (it is) a Qur'ân which We have divided (into parts), in order that you might recite it to men at intervals. And We have revealed it by stages." (*Sûrat Al-Isrâ',* 17:106)

The Prophet Muhammad ﷺ automatically would have

memorized the Qur'ânic *Ayât* (Verses) that were revealed to him and would recite them to the Companions who happened to be with him, and ordered them to write them down immediately, Muhammad ﷺ himself used to keep a copy of the revealed portions in his house. The Qur'ân, the last of Allâh's Scriptures, is divided into 114 *Sûrah* (Chapters) of unequal length. It is the first fundamental source of Islamic *Shari'ah* (laws). Allâh says:

> "A Messenger (Muhammad ﷺ) from Allâh, reciting (the Qur'ân) purified pages [purified from *Al-Bâtil* (falsehood)].Wherein are correct and straight laws from Allâh." (*Sûrat Al-Bayyinah*, 98:2,3)

Allâh revealed some of the Qur'ân in Makkah, and the rest He revealed in Al-Madinah. The Makkan Chapters deal mainly with the issues of belief such as *Tauhîd* (Oneness of Allâh), the signs of the existence of Allâh, and the Day of Resurrection. The Chapters revealed in Al-Madinah deal mainly with the issues of law, society, and governance. The Prophet ﷺ preached the Oneness of Allâh, so did all the Prophets and Messengers of Allâh before him.

Authenticity of the Qur'ân

There is no nation that has ever cared about, revered, and preserved its Divine Scripture as the Muslim *Ummah* (nation) has cared about, revered and preserved the Qur'ân. Unlike the other Divine Scriptures, the Qur'ân is not kept in the hands of a particular group or elite of the Muslims, and

for this reason it is not subject to suspicion that it might have been tampered with or altered. Rather, it has always been within the reach of all Muslims. The Prophet ﷺ commanded the Muslims to recite Qur'ânic Chapters, or Verses in their prayer. Allâh commands the Muslims to refer all their disputes to the Qur'ân for final judgement.

The Qur'ân was compiled in its final codex at a time when the early Muslims who committed it to memory were still alive. Allâh has promised to preserve it and it will be preserved until the Day of Resurrection. Allâh says:

> "Verily, We, it is We Who have sent down the *Dhikr* (i.e. the Qur'ân) and surely We will guard it (from corruption)." (*Sûrat Al-Hijr,* 15:9)

The Muslims today read and recite the Qur'ânic texts exactly as they were read and recited during the lifetime of the Prophet Muhammad ﷺ and his Companions ﷺ. Not a single letter has been added to the Qur'ân or deleted from it.

The difference between the miracles of the previous Messengers, which proved their veracity, and that of

Muhammad ﷺ is that theirs took place during the lifetime of each one of them, whereas the miracle of the Qur'ân remains effective, everlasting and challenging until the Day of Resurrection. Allâh says:

> "And this Qur'ân is not such as could ever be produced by other than Allâh (Lord of the heavens and the earth), but it is a confirmation of (the Revelation) which was before it, and a full explanation of the Book– wherein there is no doubt–from the Lord of the '*Âlamîn*. Or do they say: 'He (Muhammad ﷺ) has forged it?' Say: 'Bring then a *Sûrah* (Chapter) like unto it, and call upon whomsoever you can besides Allâh, if you are truthful!'" (*Sûrat Yûnus,* 10:37-38)

The Qur'ân Comprehensive Legislation

The Qur'ân constitutes the most comprehensive legislation of Islam on the practical level as the source of the *Shari'ah* (the Divine laws). It is comprehensive because it includes the laws as well as the underlying purposes and moral principles and the beliefs to which every Muslim must subscribe. Islamic *Shari'ah* is designed and made suitable not only for Muslims but also for all mankind for all times. The Islamic law governs all human acts, by delineating every person's public and private duties toward Allâh and His creation, including man.

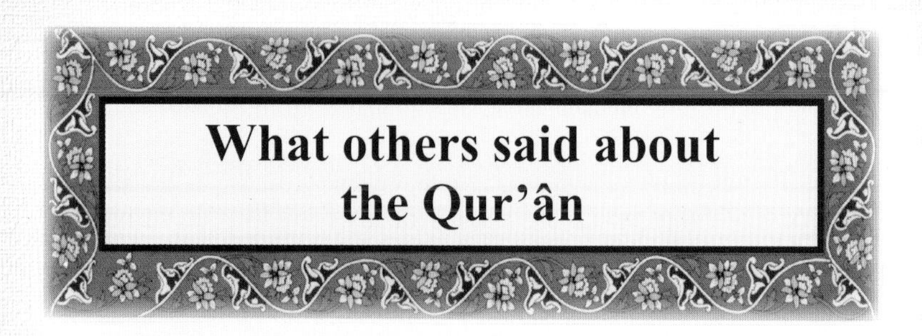

What others said about the Qur'ân

"However often we turn to it (the Qur'ân) at first disgusting us each time afresh, it soon attracts, astounds, and in the end enforces our reverence...Its style, in accordance with its contents and aim is stern, grand, terrible – ever and anon truly sublime – Thus this book will go on exercising through all ages a most potent influence."

(Goethe, Quoted in T.P. Hughes' *Dictionary of Islam,* p. 526.)

"A work, then, which calls forth so powerful and seemingly incompatible emotions even in the distant reader – distant as to time, and still more so as to mental development – a work which not only conquers the repugnance which he may begin its perusal, but changes this adverse feeling into astonishment and admiration, such a work must be a wonderful production of the human mind indeed and a problem of the highest interest to every thoughtful observer of the destinies of mankind,"

(Dr. Steingass, quoted in Huges' *Dictionary of Islam, p.* 526-27.)

"Its (the Qur'ân's) as a literary production should perhaps not be measured by some preconceived maxims of subjective and aesthetic taste, but by the effects which it produced in Muhammad's contemporaries and fellow countrymen. If it spoke so powerfully and convincingly to the hearts of his hearers as to weld hitherto centrifugal and antagonistic elements into one compact and well organized body, animated by ideas far beyond those which had until now ruled the Arabian mind, then its eloquence was perfect, simply because it created a civilized nation out of savage tribes, and shot a fresh woof into the old wrap of history." (*Ibid.* p. 528)

"A totally objective study of it [the Qur'ân] in the light of modern knowledge, leads us to recognize the agreement between the two, as has been already noted on repeated occasions. It makes us deem it quite unthinkable for a man of Muahmmad's time to have been the author of such statements, on account of the state of knowledge in his day. Such considerations are part of what gives the Qur'ânic revelation its unique place, and forces the impartial scientist to admit his inability to provide an explanation which calls solely upon materialistic reasoning."

(Maurice Bucaille. *The Qur'ân and Modern Science,* 1981, p.18)

Who is 'Îsâ (Jesus)?

Although 'Îsâ ﷺ is highly respected in Islam, Islam does not accept any concept of his divinity, or the belief that he is the son of God. This or any Trinitarian dogma concerning God or any suggesting that 'Îsâ is an incarnation, spiritual or physical, of God, is totally rejected in Islam. Allâh says:

> "O people of the Scripture (Christians)! Do not exceed the limits in your religion, nor say of Allâh aught but the truth. The Messiah 'Îsâ (Jesus), son of Maryam (Mary), was (no more than) a Messenger of Allâh and His Word, ('Be!' – and he was) which He bestowed on Maryam (Mary) and a spirit (*Rûh*) created by Him; so believe in Allâh and His Messengers. Say not: 'Three (trinity)!' Cease! (it is) better for you. For Allâh is (the only) One *Ilâh* (God), Glorified is He (Far Exalted is He) above having a son. To Him belongs all that is in the heavens and all that is in the earth. And Allâh is All-Sufficient as a Disposer of affairs."
>
> "The Messiah will never be proud to reject to be a servant of Allâh, nor the angels who are the near (to Allâh). And whosoever rejects His worship and is proud, then He will gather them all together unto Himself." (*Sûrat An-Nisâ',* 4:171,172)
>
> "Remember) when Allâh will say (on the Day of Resurrection). O 'Îsâ (Jesus), son of Maryam (Mary)!

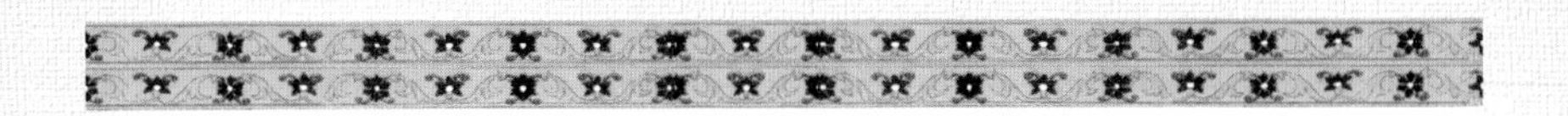

Remember My Favor to you and to your mother when I supported you with *Rûh-ul-Qudus* [Jibrîl (Gabriel)] so that you spoke to the people in the cradle and in maturity; and when I taught you writing, *Al-Hikmah* (the power of understanding), the *Taurât* (Torah) and the *Injeel* (Gospel); and when you made out of the clay, a figure like that of a bird, by My Permission, and you breathed into it, and it became a bird by My Permission, and you healed those born blind, and the lepers by My Permission, and when you brought forth the dead by My Permission; and when I restrained the Children of Israel from you (when they resolved to kill you) as you came unto them with clear proofs, and the disbelievers among them said: 'This is nothing but evident magic.'"

"And when I (Allâh) inspired *Al-Hawâriyyûn* (the disciples) [of 'Îsâ (Jesus)] to believe in Me and My Messenger, they said: 'We believe. And bear witness that we are Muslims.'"

"(Remember) when *Al-Hawâriyyûn* (the disciples) said: 'O 'Îsâ (Jesus), son of Maryam (Mary)! Can your Lord send down to us a table spread (with food) from heaven?' 'Îsâ (Jesus) said: 'Fear Allâh, if you are indeed believers.'"

"They said: 'We wish to eat thereof and to satisfy our hearts (to be stronger in Faith), and to know that you have indeed told us the truth and that we ourselves be its witnesses.'"

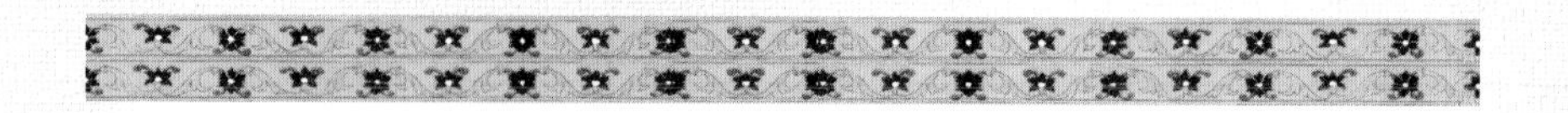

"Îsâ (Jesus), son of Maryam (Mary), said: 'O Allâh, our Lord! Send us from the heaven a table spread (with food) that there may be for us – for the first and the last of us – a festival and a sign from You; and provide us with sustenance, for You are the Best of sustainers.'"

"Allâh said: 'I am going to send it down unto you, but if any of you after that disbelieves, then I will punish him with a torment such as I have not inflicted on anyone among (all) the *'Âlamîn* (mankind and jinn).'"

"And (remember) when Allâh will say (on the Day of Resurrection): 'O 'Îsâ (Jesus), son of Maryam (Mary)! Did you say unto men: Worship me and my mother as two gods besides Allâh?' He will say: 'Glorified are You! It was not for me to say what I had no right (to say). Had I said such a thing, You would surely have known it. You know what is in my inner self though I do not know what is in Yours; truly, You, only You, are the All-Knower of all that is hidden (and unseen).'"

"Never did I say to them aught except what You (Allâh) did command me to say: 'Worship Allâh, my Lord and your Lord.' And I was a witness over them while I dwelt amongst them, but when You took me up, You were the Watcher over them; and You are a Witness to all things. (This is a great admonition and warning to the Christians of the whole world)." (*Sûrat Al-Mâidah,* 5:110-117)

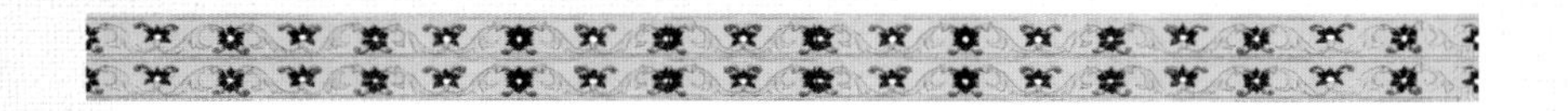

Concerning the birth of 'Îsâ ﷺ, Allâh says:

> "And mention in the Book (the Qur'ân, O Muhammad ﷺ the story of) Maryam (Mary), when she withdrew in seclusion from her family to a place facing east. She placed a screen (to screen herself) from them; then We sent to her Our *Ruh* [angel Jibrîl (Gabriel)], and he appeared before her in the form of a man in all respects. She said: 'Verily, I seek refuge with the Most Gracious (Allâh) from you, if you do fear Allâh.' (The angel) said: 'I am only a messenger from your Lord, (to announce) to you the gift of a righteous son.' She said: 'How can I have a son, when no man has touched me, nor am I unchaste? He said: 'So (it will be), your Lord said: That is easy for Me (Allâh)! And (We wish) to appoint him as a sign to mankind and a mercy from Us (Allâh), and it is a matter (already) decreed (by Allâh)."
>
> "So she conceived him, and she withdrew with him to a far place (i.e., Bethlehem valley about 4-6 miles from Jerusalem). And the pains of childbirth drove her to the trunk of a date palm. She said: 'Would that I had died before this, and has been forgotten and out of sight!' Then [the babe 'Îsâ (Jesus) or Jibrîl (Gabriel)] cried unto her from below her, saying: 'Grieve not: your Lord has provided a water stream under you. And shake the trunk of date palm towards you, it will let fall fresh ripe dates upon you. So eat and drink and be glad.

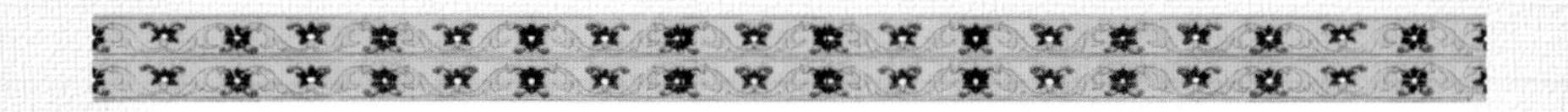

And if you see any human being, say: 'Verily, I have vowed a fast unto the Most Gracious (Allâh) so I shall not speak to any human being this day.' Then she brought him (the baby) to her people, carrying him. They said: 'O Mary! Indeed you have brought a thing *Fariyy* (a mighty thing)." (*Tafsir At-Tabari*)

"O sister (i.e., the like) of *Hârûn* (Aaron)! Your father was not a man who used to commit adultery, nor your mother was an unchaste woman. Then she pointed to him. They said: 'How can we talk to one who is a child in the cradle?' He [Îsâ (Jesus)] said: 'Verily, I am a servant of Allâh, He has given me the Scripture and made me a Prophet. And He has made me blessed wheresoever I be, and has enjoined on me *Salât* (prayer), and *Zakât*, as long as I live. And (He has made me) dutiful to my mother, and made me not arrogant, unblest. And *Salâm* (peace) be upon me the day I was born, and the day I die, and the day I shall be raised alive!' Such is 'Îsâ (Jesus), son of Maryam (Mary). (It is) a statement of truth about which they doubt (or dispute)."

"It befits not (the Majesty of) Allâh that He should beget a son [this refers to the slander of Christians against Allâh, by saying that 'Îsâ (Jesus) is the son of Allâh]. Glorified (and Exalted) is He (above all that they associate with Him). When He decrees a thing, He only says to it: 'Be'!– and it is. [Îsâ (Jesus) said:]

'And verily, Allâh is my Lord and your Lord. So worship Him (Alone). That is the Straight Path.' (Allâh's religion of Islamic Monotheism which He did ordain for all of His Prophets)." (*Sûrat Maryam*, 19:16-36)

'Îsâ عليه السلام did not die upon the cross, as commonly believed by the Christians, rather Allâh raised him up to Him. It was someone else who was actually crucified. Allâh says:

"And because of their saying (in boast), 'We killed Messiah 'Îsâ (Jesus), son of Maryam (Mary), the Messenger of Allâh,' – but they killed him not, nor crucified him, but it appeared so to them [the resemblance of 'Îsâ (Jesus) was put over another man (and they killed that man)], and those who differ therein are full of doubts. They have no (certain) knowledge, they follow nothing but conjecture. For surely they killed him not [i.e., 'Îsâ (Jesus), son of Maryam (Mary) عليه السلام]: But Allâh raised him [Îsâ (Jesus)] up (with his body and soul) unto Himself (and he عليه السلام is in the heavens). And Allâh is Ever All-Powerful, All-Wise." (*Sûrat An-Nisâ'*, 4: 157-8)

Allâh enabled 'Îsâ عليه السلام to perform certain miracles as a sign of his truth and authenticity as described in the following Verse:

"And will make him [Îsâ (Jesus)] a Messenger to the Children of Israel (saying): 'I have come to you with a sign from your Lord, that I design for you out of clay, a

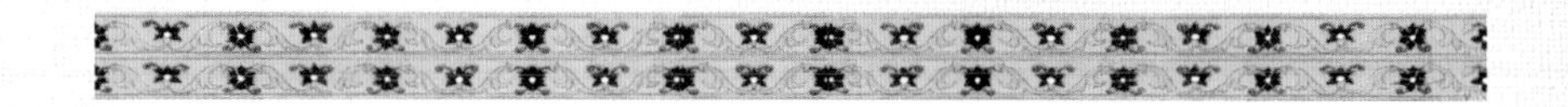

figure like that of a bird, and breathe into it, and it becomes a bird by Allâh's Leave; and I heal him who was born blind, and the leper, and I bring the dead to life by Allâh's Leave. And I inform you of what you eat, and what you store in your houses. Surely, therein is a sign for you, if you believe." (*Sûrat Al-Imran*, 3:49)

'Îsâ right now is in the heavens. He will come down to earth near to the end of time, as a major sign of the Final Hour. Allâh describes 'Îsâ saying:

"He [Îsâ (Jesus)] was not more than a servant. We granted Our Favor to him, and We made him an example for the Children of Israel (i.e. his creation without a father)." (*Sûrat Az-Zukhruf,* 43:59)

Allâh also says:

"And he [Îsâ (Jesus), son of Maryam (Mary)] shall be a known sign for (the coming of) the Hour (Day of Resurrection) [i.e.'Îsâ's descent on the earth]. Therefore have no doubt concerning it (i.e.,the Day of Resurrection). And follow Me (Allâh) (i.e. be obedient to Allâh and do what He orders you to do, O mankind!) This is the Straight Path (of Islâmic Monotheism, leading to Allâh and to His Paradise)." (*Sûrat Az-Zukhruf,* 43:61)

Allâh has created the creatures to worship Him, and provided them with provisions to enable them to do that. Allâh, the Exalted, says:

> "And I have created the jinn and men only to worship Me. I want no sustenance from them, nor do I want them to feed Me. Surely, it is Allâh Who is the Provider, the Powerful." (*Sûrat Adh-Dhâriyât*, 51: 56-58)

Man naturally acknowledges Allâh's divinity, loves Him, worships Him, and ascribes no partner to Him. But human and jinn devils who suggest to each other polished speech out of deception, corrupt his natural disposition, and lead him astray.

Tawheed[1] is firmly instilled in human nature; while polytheism is accidental and intrusive. Allâh says:

> "And remain steadfast on the *Deen*[2] *Hanifan*[3], the faith with which Allâh created mankind. There is no alteration of the *Deen* of Allâh." (*Sûrat Ar-Rûm*, 30:30)

And the Prophet ﷺ said:

---

1. The belief in the Oneness of Allâh.
2. *'Deen'* in Arabic commonly refers to a whole way of life which is based on the Book and the *Sunnah* and the exemplary application of both by the Messenger of Allâh ﷺ.
3. One who inclines from any false religion to the true *Deen* of Islam.

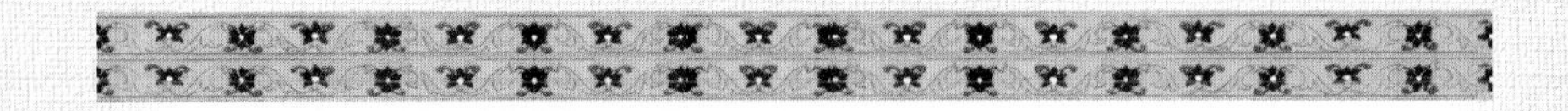

"Every infant is born with an innate disposition ,[4] but it is his parents who make him a Jew, or a Christian or a Magian."[5]

Hence, the *Tawheed* or the belief in the Oneness of Allâh is man's innate belief.

Islam is the Faith which was upheld by Adam, whom Allâh rendered safe from evil and those who came after him for many centuries. Allâh says:

"Mankind was one community, then Allâh sent the Prophets as bearers of good tidings and as warners." (*Sûrat Al-Baqarah,* 2:213)

Polytheism and doctrinal perversion appeared first among the people of Noah who was the first Messenger, Allâh sent, as proven by His words:

"We have revealed to you just as We revealed to Noah and to the Prophets after him." (*Sûrat An-Nisâ'*, 4:163)

Among the requirements of believing in Allâh, the Exalted, and worshipping Him is submitting to His Judgment, and contentement with His laws, and the referral to His Book and to the *Sunnah* of His Messenger ﷺ, in disputes with regards to statements, fundamentals, litigations, blood, properties, and the rest of rights. For Allâh is the ultimate Judge and judgment ultimately pertains to Him. It is incumbent upon the rulers to

---

4. The faculty of knowing Allâh with which man is created.
5. Bukhari & Muslim.

rule by what Allâh revealed, and it is incumbent upon the subjects to seek judgment from the Book of Allâh and the *Sunnah* of His Messenger ﷺ. With regards to rulers, Allâh says:

> "Verily, Allâh commands you to deliver the trust[6] committed to you to their due owners, and that when you judge between people, to judge with justice. And surely excellent is that with which Allâh admonishes you. Allâh is All-Hearing, All-Seeing." (*Sûrat An-Nisâ',* 4:58)

And with regards to the subjects, He said:

> "O you who believe, obey Allâh and His Messenger, and the people in authority among you. And if you dispute over anything, refer it to Allâh and His Messenger if you really believe in Allâh and the Last Day, that is best in terms of consequences." (*Sûrat An-Nisâ',* 4:59)

6. The term, 'trust' means Rights of Allâh including all of His Commands, and the rights of humans that are committed to man.

Who is Muhammad ﷺ?

Muhammad ﷺ is the last of the Prophets and Messengers whom Allâh has sent to mankind. His full name is Muhammad, son of 'Abdullâh bin 'Abdul-Muttalib bin Hâshim.

Life and Mission

He was born in Makkah in the year of the Elephant, 570 C.E. After the death of his father, 'Abdullâh, he was under the care of his grandfather, 'Abdul-Muttalib. It was the custom then to raise infants and children in a healthier environment outside the city, so he was given as a baby to a wet nurse from a nomadic tribe and spent a few years in the desert. At the age of six he lost his mother, 'Aminah of the clan of Zuhrah, and at the age of eight his grandfather, 'Abdul-Muttalib.

Muhammad ﷺ came under the care of the new head of the clan, his uncle Abu Tâlib, who took him on a successful trading journey to Syria in about 595. Soon afterwards, he went on a second trading journey in which he was in charge of the merchandise of Khadijah, a rich lady from the Quraish tribe. She was impressed by his trustworthiness and married him. She was 40, fifteen years older than he was, but she bore him two sons, who died young, and four daughters: Ruqayyah, Zainab, Umm Kulthum and Fatimah رضى الله عنهن. Fâtimah became the wife of 'Ali رضي الله عنه, the Prophet's cousin.

The Prophetic Mission

The Prophet Muhammad ﷺ was in the habit of occasionally spending nights in a mountain cave near Makkah. Makkah was inhabited by the tribe of Quraish, to which the Hâshim clan belonged, it was a mercantile center formed around the Sacred House, the Ka'bah, which was a sanctuary for all and assured the safety of those who used to frequent it. About the year 610, the Prophet ﷺ received the first Divinely revealed Verses of the Qur'ân through the angel, Jibreel (Gabriel).

Allâh says:

> "Read! In the Name of your Lord Who has created (all that exists). He has created man from a clot (a piece of thick coagulated blood). Read! And your Lord is the Most Generous. Who has taught (the writing) by the pen. He has taught man that which he knew not. (*Sûrat Al-'Alaq*, 96:1-5)

Jibreel (Gabriel) told him, "You are the Messenger of Allâh." From this time, at frequent intervals until his death, he

received Revelations that came to him directly from Allâh, which were written down. At a later stage they were collected into a book, i.e., the Qur'ân which has endured unchanged until today. The Qur'ân contains the actual Words of Allâh Himself.

Khadijah's Christian cousin verified these Revelations to be identical with those sent by Allâh to Moses and Jesus عليهم السلام.

From the first vision and Revelation, he was told to communicate them to the people.

Allâh says:

> "O you (Muhammad ﷺ) enveloped in garments! Arise and warn! And magnify your Lord (Allâh)!" (*Al-Muddaththir*, 74:1-3)

Soon some of his close acquaintances who believed in him accepted Islam. Later on, he began preaching publicly, and the Prophet ﷺ and his followers used to spend their days together in the house of Al-Arqam. The people of Makkah at the time were pagans worshipping idols. By proclaiming his message publicly, the Prophet ﷺ gained more followers, mostly young men, before there appeared opposition to the new faith. The new believers included sons and brothers of the richest men in Makkah while others were considered as "weak," which meant they had no tribal standing and were not protected by any clan.

This new Faith (*Deen*) was Islam, which means submission to God, Allâh the All-Mighty; and its adherents are Muslims, those submitting to Allâh.

Opposition at Makkah

Opposition became active when the Prophet ﷺ began condemning idol worship and declared the creed of *Tauheed* (the belief in the Oneness of Allâh).

> "And when they see you (O Muhammad ﷺ), they treat you only in mockery (saying): 'Is this the one whom Allâh has sent as a Messenger?' He would have nearly misled us from our *âlihah* (gods), had it not been that we were patient and constant in their worship! And they will know, when they see the torment, who it is that is most astray from the (Right) Path!" (*Sûrat Al-Furqân,* 25:41,42)

A leader of the opposition arose in the person of Abu Jahl, who organized a boycott against the Hâshim clan by the chief clans of Makkah because they continued to protect the Prophet ﷺ and did not stop him from preaching.

Both Khadijah رضى الله عنها, the wife of the Prophet ﷺ and his uncle Abu Tâlib died about 619. Allâh's Messenger ﷺ continued preaching among other tribes and went to Tâ'if to invite its tribes to accept

his Message, but they refused to accept. In 620 Allâh's Messenger ﷺ came in touch with clans from Al-Madinah, leading to emigration, *Hijrah*, in 622.

The persecution led some Muslims in about 615 to emigrate to Ethiopia, some of whom remained there until 628, long after the Prophet ﷺ was established in Al-Madinah.

The Emigration

In the summer of 612 C.E, twelve men from Al-Madinah, visited Makkah for the annual pilgrimage. They secretly met the Prophet ﷺ, accepted Islam and went back to Al-Madinah, and propagated Islam there. At the pilgrimage, a few years later, a representative party of 75 men from Al-Madinah including two women not only accepted Islam but also took an oath to obey and defend the Prophet ﷺ as they would their own kin. These are known as the two pledges of *'Al-Aqabah*. The Prophet ﷺ now encouraged his faithful followers to make their way to Al-Madinah in small groups.

The Companions of Allâh's Messenger ﷺ left for Al-Madinah, but he ﷺ stayed in Makkah waiting for Divine permission to migrate. None of his Companions stayed behind except for Abu Bakr and 'Ali رضى الله عنهما, and those Muslims under restraint and those who were forced to apostatize.

The Quraish saw that the Messenger of Allâh ﷺ had a following, from their tribe plus companions from other tribes and they were all outside the territory of the Quraish. When they had settled in their new home in Al-Madinah, and had gained protection, the Quraish feared that the Prophet ﷺ might join them and get away from their control. So they plotted to kill the Prophet ﷺ by assigning a group of young men, one from each clan, to execute their plan. But Jibreel instructed him not to sleep in his bed the night, the plan was to take place. Before much of that night had passed, they assembled outside his door waiting for him to sleep. When the Prophet ﷺ saw them, he went out with a handful of dust without them seeing him, as a Divine miracle, and sprinkled the dust on their heads and went on his way. They entered his room and found 'Ali ﷺ lying in his bed and mistook him for the Prophet ﷺ. When 'Ali ﷺ came out in the morning, after they had waited in ambush all night, they realized their folly.

The Prophet ﷺ told 'Ali to stay behind so he could return the valuables that people had entrusted to the Prophet ﷺ, he being renown for his honesty. The Prophet ﷺ came to Abu Bakr ﷺ, his closest Companion, and they escaped from Makkah to a cave in Thaur, a mountain near Makkah. They remained there for three days, Abu Bakr's son and daughter supplied them with news and provisions.

When the Quraish realized that the Prophet ﷺ had escaped, they offered a reward of one hundred camels to anyone who would bring him back. Finally, two camels were brought for them and they rode off. They reached Quba, a suburb of Al-Madinah, on the 12th of Rabi'-ul-Awwal. His Companions went out to receive him, everyone was excited and joyful. He stayed in Quba for four days, then in Al-Madinah, he laid the foundation of his mosque and his own living quarters. The arrival of the Prophet ﷺ is the traditional starting point of the Islamic calendar, on that day he was 53 years old in the year 622 of the Western calendar. The oasis of Al-Madinah is different from Makkah, in it date palms and grains are grown.

The First *Khutbah*

In the first *Khutbah*[7] of the *Jumu'ah* prayer which Allâh's Messenger ﷺ delivered, he said:

> "O men, keep in stock good deeds for yourselves. You know, by Allâh, that everyone of you will die, and will leave his sheep without a shepherd. Then his Lord will ask him with no interpreter in between; 'Did not my Messenger come to you, and did not I give you wealth and favor you with My Bounty?' What have you accomplished for yourselves? Then one of you will look to the right and see nothing, and to the left and see nothing. Then he will look in front of him and see nothing but Hell. He who can protect himself from Fire even by

7. *Khutbah*, an Islamic term for a formal religious speech usually delivered prior to *Jumu'ah* (Friday) Prayer.

giving in charity a piece of a date fruit, then let him do so, and he who cannot find that, then give a good word, for a good deed will be rewarded tenfold and up to seven hundred fold."

"Two major tribes occupied Al-Madinah: The Aus and the Khazraj who coexisted with three Jewish tribes. Just as the Prophet ﷺ had established a code of brotherhood amongst the believers, so too he was keen on establishing friendly relations between the Muslims and non-Muslim tribes of Arabia. He established a sort of treaty aiming at ruling out all pre-Islamic rancor and intertribal feuds. He was so meticulous not to leave any area in the charter that would allow pre-Islamic traditions to sneak in or violate the new environment he wanted to establish.

It was solely by his wisdom and dexterity, that the Prophet ﷺ erected the pillars of the new society. This phenomenon no doubt left its mark on the virtuous Muslims. He used to bring them up in the light of the Islamic education, he sanctified their selves, enjoined them to observe righteousness and praiseworthy manners and was keen on infusing into them the ethics of amity, glory, honor, worship and first and foremost obedience to Allâh and His Messenger ﷺ.

The Prophet ﷺ had drafted the famous document, which was known as the Constitution of Al-Madinah. It created a confederation of the native Al-Madinah tribes and the emigrants from Makkah. It is stated that all disputes were to be referred to the Prophet ﷺ.

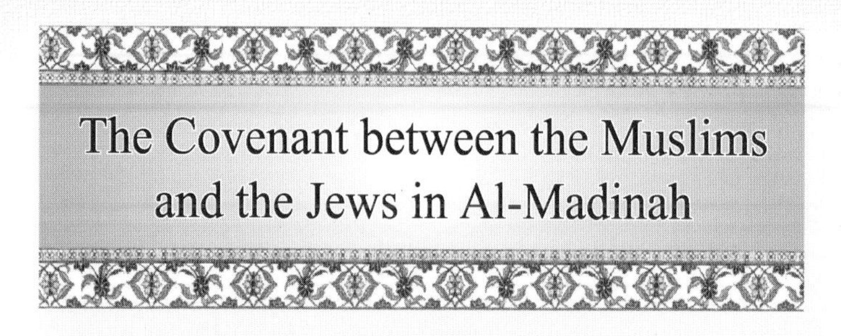

The Covenant between the Muslims and the Jews in Al-Madinah

Allâh's Messenger ﷺ composed a document concerning the *Muhâjirin* (emigrants of Makkah) and the *Ansâr* (the residents of Al-Madinah) in which he made a friendly agreement with the Jews and acknowledged their religion and their property and stated the reciprocal obligations, as follows:

> I begin with the Name of Allâh, the Most Gracious, the Most Merciful.
>
> This is a document from Muhammad, the Prophet (governing the relations) between the believers and Muslims of both Quraish and Yathrib, and those who follow them, join them, and fight alongside them. They are one *Ummah* (community) to the exclusion of all men.[8]
>
> The *Muhâjirin* from Quraish, according to their prevalent customs, shall pay the blood money among themselves; and shall ransom their captives with kindness and fairness common among believers.
>
> Banu 'Auf according to their present custom, shall pay the blood money they used to pay in the past; every

8. The statement 'to the exclusion of all men' signifies that the treaty applied exclusively to the *Muhâjirin*, the *Ansâr*, and the Jews of Al-Madinah.

party shall ransom its captives with kindness and fairness common among believers.

Banu Sâ'idah, according to their present custom, shall pay the blood money they used to pay in the past; every party shall ransom its captives with kindness and fairness common among believers.

Banu Al-Hârith, according to their present custom, shall pay the blood money they used to pay in the past; every party shall ransom its captives with kindness and fairness common among believers.

And Banu Jusham, according to their present custom, shall pay the blood money they used to pay in the past; every party shall ransom its captives with kindness and fairness common among believers.

And Banu An-Najjâr likewise.[9]

Banu 'Amr bin 'Auf, Banu An-Nabit and Banu Al-Aus likewise.[10]

And the believers shall help one who is overburdened

9. These all belong to Al-Khazraj.
10. These all belong to Al-Aus.

by debt (of a ransom or blood money) among them to pay off his debt.

No believer shall take as an ally the freedman of another believer against him.

The God-fearing believers shall stand against the rebellious or him who seeks to oppress, or commits a wrongful doing, or transgresses, or promotes corruption among believers; the hand of every man shall be against him even if he be a son of one of them. A believer shall not slay a believer in retaliation for a disbeliever, nor shall he aid a disbeliever against a believer. The protection of Allâh is one, the common of them may give protection to a stranger on their behalf.

The believers are friends and supporters one to the other to the exclusion of outsiders. The Jews who follow us would be helped and would be treated equitably. They shall not be wronged nor shall their enemies be aided against them.

The peace treaty shall include all believers. No peace should include some believers and exclude others while they are warring in the cause of Allâh. Fighting in the cause of Allâh is on fair and equitable conditions to all. In every raid, a rider must take another behind him.

The believers must avenge the blood of one another shed in the way of Allâh.

The God-fearing believers enjoy the best and most upright guidance.

No polytheist[11] shall grant protection to the property or a person of the Quraish, nor shall he intervene against a believer. Whosoever is convicted of killing a believer without legal reason, shall be subject to retaliation unless the guardian of the slain (the next of kin) is satisfied (with blood money), and the believers shall be against him as one man, and they are bound to take action against him.

It shall not be lawful to a believer who holds by what is in this document and believes in Allâh and the Last Day, to harbor and protect a *Muhdith*.[12] The curse of Allâh and His anger on the Day of Resurrection will be upon him who supports and harbors him. Neither repentance nor ransom will be accepted from him. Whenever you differ about a matter, it must be referred to Allâh and to Muhammad.

The Jews shall contribute to the cost of war so long as they are fighting alongside the believers. The Jews of Banu 'Auf are one community with the believers (the Jews have their religion and the Muslims have theirs), their freedmen and their persons except those who

11. Presumably the heathen Arabs of Al-Madinah are referred to.
12. *Muhdith*, a person innovating religious practices, a criminal or an offender.

behave unjustly and sinfully, for they hurt none but themselves and their families. The same applies to the Jews of An-Najjâr, Al-Hârith, Banu Sâ'idah, Banu Jusham, Banu Al-Aus, Banu Tha'labah, and Jafna, a clan of the Tha'labah. The close friends of the Jews are regarded as themselves. None of them shall go out to war except with the permission of Muhammad, but he shall not be prevented from taking revenge for a wound. He who slays a man without warning, slays himself and his household, unless it be one who has wronged him, for Allâh will accept that. The Jews must bear their expenses and the Muslims their expense. Each must help the other against anyone who attacks the people of this document. They must seek mutual advice and consultation, and loyalty is a protection against treachery.

A man is not liable for his ally's misdeeds. The wronged must be helped. The Jews must pay with the believers so long as war lasts. Yathrib shall be inviolable for the people of this document. A stranger under protection shall be as his host doing no harm and committing no crime. A woman shall only be given protection with the consent of her family. If any dispute or controversy likely to cause trouble should arise, it must be referred to Allâh and to Muhammad, the Messenger of Allâh. Allâh accepts what is nearest

to piety and goodness in this document. (The pagans of) Quraish and their helpers shall not be given protection. The contracting parties are bound to help one another against any attack on Yathrib. If they are called to make peace and maintain it, they must do so; and if they make a similar demand on the Muslims, it must be carried out except in the case of fighting for the religion (*Deen*). Every one shall have his protection from the side to which he belongs; the Jews of Al-Aus, their freedmen and themselves have the same standing with the people of this document in sheer loyalty from the people of this document.

Loyalty is a protection against treachery: he who acquires a thing acquires it for himself. Allâh approves of this document. This document will not protect the unjust and the sinner.

The Jews refused to acknowledge Muhammad ﷺ as Prophet. Most of the Arabs in Al-Madinah were Muslims, who recognized him as the only authority in all aspects of life.

The Prophet ﷺ used as well to promote the habit of abstention from asking others for help unless one is totally helpless. He used to talk to his Companions a lot about the merits, virtues and Divine reward implied in observing the prescribed worships and rituals. He would always bring forth corroborated proofs in order to link them physically and spiritually to the Revelation sent to him, hence he would apprise them of their duties and responsibilities in terms of

the consequences of the Call of Islam, and at the same time emphasize the exigencies of comprehension and contemplation.

That was his practice of maximizing their morale and imbuing them with noble values and ideals so that they could become models of virtue to be copied by subsequent generations.

The Early Years in Al-Madinah

The first year was spent in settling down. Although the majority of the Arabs were Muslims, some of them were not interested in Islam. Because they were outnumbered by the Muslims, and they had to coexist with them without being able to manage on their own, they had no choice but to join in by pretending to be Muslims. This category was known as hypocrites.

The Jews whose interests clashed with Islam, had many things in common with the hypocrites, so they joined hands in plotting against Islam. Many a time the hypocrites would decline to participate in military expeditions and battles against the pagan Arabs.

In the meantime, Allâh the Exalted gave the believers the permission to fight their enemies and the polytheists who were nearby. This was thirteen years after the Prophet ﷺ was commanded to speak to the people.

Almost a year after his arrival, the Prophet ﷺ went forth on his first military expedition. He raided the people of Al-Abwa who were heading for the Quraish. The people of Al-Abwa made peace with him and he returned to Al-Madinah without engaging in combat. After this Allâh's Messenger ﷺ dispatched expeditions on regular intervals some of which he

led himself.

In the month of Ramadân, March 624, Allâh's Messenger ﷺ heard that Abu Sufyân, the head of the Umaiyad clan was coming from Syria with a wealthy Makkan caravan of the Quraish accompanied by thirty or forty men. The Prophet ﷺ summoned the Muslims and went with 315 men to intercept it.

Having taken alarm, Abu Sufyân sent a man to call the Quraish in defense of their property and to tell them that Muhammad ﷺ and his Companions were lying in wait for the caravan. Upon hearing this news the Quraish set out to fight the Prophet ﷺ and his Companions.

Abu Sufyân managed to elude the Muslims by taking different routes. When he saw that he had saved the caravan, he sent a word to Quraish to return to Makkah, but their leaders refused and insisted upon war and marched forth with 900 men and reached a place near Badr where they camped.

The battle started with individual duels, then fighting became fierce. The leaders of Quraish fell one after another along with 45 of their men who were killed including Abu Jahl, and 70 of them were taken as prisoners, while 14 Muslims were killed. This flash victory was a Divine vindication of Muhammad's Prophethood, and he ﷺ and his Companions were greatly elated.

When the Prophet ﷺ had finished with the enemy, he ordered

that the dead of the pagans be thrown into a pit. The news of the great victory reached the people of Al-Madinah and was met with jubilation. Allâh's Messenger ﷺ and his Companions arrived in Al-Madinah bringing along with them the captives, while the Quraish returned home to wail for their dead. Many captives ransomed themselves or their Makkan relatives sent ransom money for them.

The victory in Badr had weakened the Muslim's most serious opponents in Al-Madinah, the hypocrites (the *Munâfiqun*) or nominal Muslims whose allies were the Jews. Thus, the victory of Badr strengthened the Muslims. After the Battle of Badr, Allâh's Messenger ﷺ summoned the Jewish clan of Banu Qainuqâ' in their market place and said to them:

> "O Jews beware lest Allâh brings upon you the vengeance as He brought upon the Quraish. Accept Islam, you know I am the Prophet whose description is mentioned in your Scripture."

They refused to admit it and were defiant. Thereupon Allâh revealed the following:

> "Say (O Muhammad ﷺ) to those who disbelieve: You will be vanquished and summoned to Hell, an evil resting place. You have already had a lesson in two forces that met, one force fought in the cause of Allâh. And the other were disbelievers."(*Sûrat Âl 'Imrân*, 3:12,13)

Banu Qainuqâ' were the first Jews to break their agreement with Allâh's Messenger ﷺ. Allâh's Messenger ﷺ besieged them until they surrendered unconditionally.

When Quraish suffered their defeat at Badr, they used the revenue of Abu Sufyân's caravan to finance another expedition against the Muslims in Al-Madinah to avenge their dead at Badr. So they mobilized the Makkans and their allies in the year 625 and reached the outskirts of Al-Madinah with 3000 men.

When Allâh's Messenger ﷺ heard about their march, he went out to meet them and stationed his 700 troops at a high ground on mount Uhud. The next morning, the pagans waged their attack but were repulsed with considerable loss by the Muslim archers. As the Muslims pursued, the pagan cavalry launched a flank attack after the archers left their positions and the Muslims were thrown into confusion. Some made for a fort and were cut down, but the Prophet ﷺ and the bulk of his force managed to gain the lower slopes of Mount Uhud. There they were safe from the pagan cavalry. The pagans because of their losses, were unable to press home their advantages and without delay set out for home.

Allah's Messenger ﷺ returned along with his troops to Al-Madinah. The next day he went after the pagans who themselves thought of returning to the Muslims but were disheartened by the news of the Muslims marching towards them.

The Battle of Uhud, although the pagans killed many Muslims, did not produce the decisive victory they had hoped for, neither did it deal the Muslims a crippling defeat, it was only a temporary military reversal, and soon the Muslims regained confidence and high morale.

For two years after the Battle of Uhud, the Muslim's position was strengthened through expeditions led by Allâh's Messenger ﷺ himself or those that he sanctioned. Such military activities also helped to extend the Prophet's alliances and prevent others from joining the Makkan pagans.

Pursuant to their plot against his life, the Prophet ﷺ raided the Jews of Banu An-Nadir who were deceived by false promises of support by the hypocrites of Al-Madinah. They succumbed and asked the Messenger ﷺ to spare their lives and let them leave allowing them to take with them their movable property excluding their armor to which he agreed.

In the 5th year of *Hijrah* 627, a number of Jews who had formed a party against the Muslims, went to the Quraish in Makkah and proposed a joint attack against the Muslims. The Quraish who had suffered losses and humiliation at the hands of the Muslims, welcomed the idea and mobilized 10,000 men and marched under the command of Abu Sufyân hoping to crush the Muslims.

When Allah's Messenger ﷺ heard the news, he ordered a trench to be dug around Al-Madinah and worked at it himself encouraging the Muslims who all worked together on it.

By the time the trench was dug, the Quraish arrived and encamped just outside Al-Madinah and besieged the Muslims for a fortnight. Attempts to cross the trench failed, and fodder for their horses grew scarce. The Prophet's agents fomented dissension between his enemies, they were successful and the Jews broke their relations with the Makkan pagans, and so did the other Arab tribes.

After many days of the hopeless siege, on a night of cold wind and rain, Abu Sufyan decided to return home. He gave up the hope of dislodging the Prophet ﷺ whose position was now greatly strengthened. The Prophet ﷺ informed the Muslims that the Quraish would not attack them after that year, and that they would attack the Quraish. The Quraish never attacked after that. It were the Muslims who attacked the Quraish when they conquered Makkah.

The hypocrites of Al-Madinah were trying hard to destabilize

the Islamic state in Al-Madinah. They abandoned the Prophet ﷺ and the Muslims at the Battle of Uhud and collaborated with the Jews whose ultimate goal was to put an end to the Prophet ﷺ and his Companions.

By joining the Confederates against the Muslims, the Jews of Banu Quraizah broke their alliance with the Prophet ﷺ and subjected themselves to a fatal end.

In the six months following the attack on Banu Quraizah, the Prophet ﷺ raided a number of Arab tribes.

The Armistice

In the 6th year after the *Hijrah*, 628 by the Western calendar, the Prophet ﷺ decided to perform '*Umrah* and took with him the *Muhâjirin* and the *Ansâr* and encamped in a place called Al-Hudaibiyah. The Quraish who feared further humiliation, decided not to allow the Prophet ﷺ or his Companions to enter Makkah lest the Arabs think that Muslims entered it by force. They sent their representative to inform him of their decision. After a few days, the Prophet ﷺ sent 'Uthmân ؓ to Makkah as his envoy. But soon it was rumored that the pagans killed him. Upon hearing this, Allâh's Messenger ﷺ took his men's pledge to remain firm and retaliate. The pledge is known as *Bai'at-ur-Ridwân* or 'The Pleasing Pledge,' because Allâh revealed words expressing His Pleasure with those who gave their pledge to His Messenger ﷺ. The rumor proved false and the Quraish delegation made a peace treaty with Allâh's Messenger ﷺ. Hostilities were to cease, and the Muslims were to be allowed to perform pilgrimage in the following year 629.

Although some of the Prophet's Companions were hoping for an engagement with the Quraish, their orderly withdrawal showed how submissive the Muslims were to the commands

of Allâh and the commands of His Messenger ﷺ. The treaty gave the freedom of choice to whoever wants to become a Muslim or simply to align himself with Allâh's Messenger ﷺ. Meanwhile the Quraish's power was in decline. Several prominent men had emigrated to Al-Madinah and accepted Islam and humiliated the Quraish even more.

Although the Quraish enjoyed the peace treaty in the safety of their caravans, they did not realize that the treaty helped increase the number of Muslims. The treaty reads as follows:

> "This is what Muhammad bin 'Abdullâh has agreed with Suhail bin 'Amr (the representative of the Quraish). They have agreed to lay aside war for ten years, during which people can be safe and abandon hostile activities on condition that if anyone from Quraish goes over to Muhammad without the permission of his guardian, he would send him back, and if anyone of Muhammad's people come to the

Quraish they would not send him back. We will not show enmity against one another, and there shall be no secret reservation or bad faith. He who wishes to enter into a pact and alliance with Muhammad may do so, and he who wishes to enter into a pact and alliance with Quraish may do so."

Thereupon the Khuzâ'ah tribe entered into a pact with the Allâh's Messenger ﷺ while the Banu Bakr went to the Quraish's side. The Quraish informed Allâh's Messenger ﷺ that he and his men should keep away from Makkah that year but to return in the following year and stay in Makkah for only three days.

The Companions of the Messenger ﷺ had no doubt about conquering Makkah because of the vision that the Prophet ﷺ saw of himself entering the House of Allâh as a conqueror. However, when they saw the negotiations for peace seemingly more favorable for the Quraish, they felt depressed. On the way back, Allâh revealed to him *Surat Al-Fath* (The Conquest) which begins:

"We have given you plain victory that Allâh forgives your past and future sins, and completes His favor upon you, and guides you to a straight path." (*Sûrat Al-Fath,* 48:1-2)

Then Allâh made it clear that He was pleased with those who gave their pledge to His Messenger ﷺ saying:

"Those who give their pledge to you, are in fact giving pledge to Allâh. The Hand of Allâh is above those..." (*Sûrat Al-Fath,* 48:10)

Banu Bakr, an ally of Quraish waged an attack against the tribe of Khuzâ'ah, an ally of Allâh's Messenger ﷺ thus violating the armistice, which led Allâh's Messenger ﷺ to denounce the treaty. After secret preparation, Allâh's Messenger ﷺ marched on Makkah a year later with 10,000 men. Abu Sufyân and other Makkan leaders went out to meet him, and formally submitted. Allah's Messenger ﷺ promised a general amnesty. When he entered Makkah, there was virtually no resistance. Only two Muslims and 28 pagans were killed, a number of people who were treacherous to the Muslims were specifically excluded from the amnesty, but even some of them were later pardoned. Thus, Allah's Messenger ﷺ who had left Makkah as a persecuted Prophet, not only entered it again in triumph but also gained the allegiance of most of the Makkans. Although he did not force them to become Muslims, the majority soon did so.

The Prophet ﷺ spent about 18 days in Makkah settling various administrative matters. The Ka'bah was cleared from idols and so was the rest of Makkah.

After the conquest of Makkah, the Battle of Hunain took place during which a stubborn enemy was finally routed. Allâh's Messenger ﷺ and the Muslims became well established in the Arabian Peninsula, most of the Arab tribes sent deputations to Al-Madinah accepting Islam.

Those Companions who were upset for having returned

home without performing *'Umrah* the previous year, now were able to see the great wisdom of the peace treaty of Al-Hudaibiyah. It was only later on when people came into Islam *en masse*, that they appreciated the vitality of this armistice.

Imam Zuhri, a renowned commentator on the *Seerah* (the Biography of the Prophet ﷺ) commented on this great event saying:

> "No victory in Islam was greater than this. There was nothing but war when people met but when there was an armistice and war stopped, people met, with a sense of security. There was none to whom Islam was explained, but embraced it. In those two years, the number of those who entered Islam doubled or more than doubled."

Ibn Hisham, the biographer of the *Seerah*, confirmed Zuhri's comment saying:

> "Allah's Messenger ﷺ went to Al-Hudaibiyah with 1400 men, then in the year of the conquest of Makkah – two years later – the Messenger ﷺ marched with 10,000 men."[13]

13. *Seerat Ibn Hishâm*, Vol. 3, p.333

The Farewell Pilgrimage

In the year 632, the Prophet ﷺ prepared to perform pilgrimage and ordered people to get ready to accompany him. It is said that 70,000 to 100,000 people performed pilgrimage with him. The Prophet ﷺ delivered on that occasion a speech that is known as the Farewell Address, for he opened it with the words:

"O people, lend me an attentive ear, for I don't know whether, after this year, I shall ever be amongst you again.

"O people listen to me! Verily your blood and your property are as sacred and inviolable as the sacredness of this day of yours, in this month of yours, in this town of yours. Behold! Everything pertaining to the Days of Ignorance is under my feet completely abolished. Abolished is also the blood revenge of the days of ignorance. The first claim of ours on blood revenge, which I abolish, is that of the son of Rabi'ah bin Al-Hârith, who was nursed among the tribe of Sa'd and killed by Hudhail. And the usury of the pre-Islamic period is abolished, and the first of our usury abolished is that of Abbâs bin Abdul-Muttalib, for it is all abolished.

"Fear Allâh concerning women. Verily, you have taken them on the security of Allâh, and intercourse with them has been made lawful unto you by Words of Allâh. You too have rights over them, and that they should not allow anyone to sit on your bed that you do not like. But if they do that, you can castigate them but not severely. Their rights upon you are that you should provide them with food and clothing in a fitting manner. I have left among you the Book of Allâh, and if you hold fast to it, you would never go astray. And you will be asked about me (on the Day of Resurrection), (now tell me) what will you say?" They (the audience) said: "We will bear witness that you have conveyed (the Message), discharged (the ministry of Prophethood) and given wise (sincere) counsel."

He (the narrator) said: He (the Prophet ﷺ) then raised his forefinger towards the sky and pointing it at the people

(said): "O Allâh, be witness. O Allâh, be witness," saying it thrice. (*Sahih Muslim*, the Book of *Hajj*: 147)

> **"Time has taken its original shape which it had when Allâh created the heavens and the earth. The year is of twelve months, four of which are sacred, and out of these (four) three are in succession, i.e., Dhul-Qa'dah, Dhul-Hijjah and Al-Muharram, and the fourth is Rajab which is named after the Mudar tribe, between (the month of) Jumâda (Ath-Thâniyah) and Sha'bân."**

Then he said, "Which month is this?" We replied, "Allâh and His Messenger know better." On that the Prophet ﷺ kept quiet so long that we thought he might name it with another name. Then the Prophet ﷺ said, "Isn't it the month of Dhul-Hijjah?" We replied, "Yes (it is)." Then he said, "Which town is this?" We replied, "Allâh and His Messenger know better." He kept quiet so long that we thought that he might name it

with another name. Then he said, "Isn't it the day of *An-Nahr* (i.e., sacrifice)?" We replied, "Yes (it is)." He said:

> "So your blood and your properties and your honor are sacred to one another like the sanctity of this day of yours, in this town of yours, in this months of yours. Surely, you will meet your Lord, and He will ask you about your deeds. Beware! Do not become like those who went astray (as infidels) after me, cutting the necks of one another. It is incumbent on those who are present to convey this message (of mine) to those who are absent. Maybe some of those to whom it will be conveyed might comprehend (what I have said) better than the present audience."

The subnarrator, Muhammad, on remembering that narration, used to say, "Muhammad spoke the truth!" He (i.e., the Prophet ﷺ) then said twice, "No doubt! Haven't I conveyed (Allâh's Message) to you?" (*Sahih Al-Bukhâri:* 4406)

The Prophet ﷺ completed the *Hajj* showing people its rites, and its procedure. Shortly after he returned to Al-Madinah, he mobilized an army to dispatch to Syria.

The Prophet ﷺ returned to Al-Madinah, aware that he was near the end of his mission, and he spent most of his time praising and glorifying Allâh who had given him success after success during his twenty-three years of Prophethood. People were entering Islam in multitudes, and delegations continued to arrive before him.

During the same time, the Prophet ﷺ sent envoys to Arab and non-Arab kings and heads of states inviting them to Islam, while military expeditions continued. In the meantime, the Prophet ﷺ began to suffer from the illness to which he succumbed four months after he returned from his Farewell Pilgrimage.

In Rabi' Al-Awwal of 11 A.H.,the Prophet ﷺ sent Usamah bin Zayad ؓ with seven hundred soldiers to the territory of Balqa and Darum in Palestine. They were to stage a show of might against the Romans, who had resumed their hostile acts. The army set out and at Jarf, only three miles outside of Al-Madihah, they received news that the Prophet ﷺ was very ill. They encamped there awaiting further news of the Prophet's health. With the Prophet's subsequent death, Usamah ؓ and his men went on with their expedition and became the first people to lead a military expedition during the Caliphate of Abu Bakr Siddeeq ؓ.

Signs of the Prophet's imminent Death

The death of Allah's Messenger ﷺ was a great catastrophe to the Muslims.

When the pangs of death started, the Prophet's strength began to decline. 'Âishah رضى الله عنها, her wife, was holding him. Just at that moment, her brother Abdur Rahmân entered the room, holding a root (*Miswaak*) used to clean teeth, 'Âishah saw the Prophet ﷺ looking at the *Miswaak*, so she asked him if he wanted it, and he nodded. She took it, and after chewing the end a little to soften it, she gave it to him.

A bowl of water was kept near the Prophet ﷺ. And he dipped both his hands into it and wiped his face, saying, "There is no God but Allâh. Verily, these are the pangs of death."

He either lifted up his hands or pointed his forefinger toward heaven, His voice was weak, but 'Âishah رضى الله عنها could hear him speak as he raised his eyes and repeated three times:

> "With the blessed from among the Prophets, the ever truthful, the martyrs, and the righteous! O Allâh, forgive me and have mercy on me. I choose to be with the exalted companions! O Allâh, the exalted companions!"

The Companions' concern over the Prophet's Death

The great (loss) news was soon known by everybody in Al-Madinah. Dark grief spread in all areas and horizons of Al-Madinah. Anas, a Companion of the Prophet ﷺ said:

"I have never witnessed a day better or brighter than that on which Allah's Messenger ﷺ came to us; and I have never witnessed a more awful or darker day than that one on which the Messenger of Allâh ﷺ died on."

When he died, his daughter, Fatimah رضى الله عنها said:

"O father, whom his Lord responded to his supplication! O father, whose abode is Paradise. O father, whom I announce his death to Gabriel." (*Sahih Al-Bukhari*, 2/641)

Biblical Prophecy on the Advent of the Prophet Muhammad ﷺ

John 14:15-16 –

> "If your love me, keep my commandments. And I will pray the Father and He shall give you another Comforter that he may abide with you forever."

Muslim theologians have said that "another Comforter" is Muhammad, the Messenger of Allâh; and him to "abide forever" means the perpetuity of his laws and way of life (*Shari'ah*) and the Book (Qur`ân) which was revealed to him.

John 15: 26-27–

> "But when the Comforter is come, whom I will send unto you from the Father, even the Spirit of truth, which proceedeth from the Father, he shall testify of me: And ye also shall bear witness, because ye have been with me from the beginning."

John 16:5-8 –

> "But now I go my way to Him that sent me and none of you asketh me 'Whither goest thou?' But because I have said these things unto you, sorrow hath filled

your heart. Nevertheless I tell you the truth; for if I go not away, the Comforter will not come unto you; but if I depart, I will send him unto you. And when he is come, he will reprove the world of sin, and approve righteousness and judgment."

John 16: 12-14 –

" I have yet many things to say unto you, but you cannot bear them now. How be it when he, the Spirit of turth, is come, he will guide you into all truth: for he shall not speak of himself; but whatsoever he shall hear, that shall he speak; and he will you things to come. He shall glorify me: for he shall receive of mine, and he shall shew it unto you."

John 16:16 –

"A little while and ye shall not see me: and again a little while, ye shall see me, because I go to the Father."

Muslim theologians have stated that the person who is described by Jesus to come after him in the above verses does not comply with any other person but Muhammad ﷺ the

Messenger of Allâh. This 'person' whom Jesus prophesied will come after him is called in the Bible 'Parqaleeta' This word was deleted by later interpreters and translators and changed at times to 'Spirit of Turth', and at other times, to 'Comforter' and sometimes to 'Holy Spirit'. The original word is Greek and its meaning is 'one whom people praise exceedingly.' The sense of the word is applicable to the word 'Muhammad' (in Arabic).

The Prophet's Features and Character

The Prophet's physical appearance was described in detail by his Companions:

The Prophet's Face

The Prophet's face was fair, attractive and round. Whenever he was pleased, his face shone bright like the full moon, but it would turn crimson when he was angry.

Al-Bara' ﷺ said: "He had the most handsome face and the best character." When he was asked: "Was the Messenger's face sword-like?" "No," He said, "it was moon-like." But in another version: he said, "His face was round." Rabi' bint Muawwidh رضى الله عنها said: "Had you seen him, you would have felt that the sun was shining." Jâbir bin Samurah ﷺ said, "I saw him on one night of the full moon. I looked at him. He was dressed in a radish garment. I compared him with the moon and found that, for me he was better than the moon." (*Mishkât Al-Masâbih,* 2: 518)

If sweat appeared on his face, the beads glistened like pearls, and the fragrance of his perspiration excelled the smell of musk.

The Prophet's cheeks were soft, his forehead wide, and his eyebrows thin and arched. His eyes were wide, with black pupils, while the whites were mixed with crimson. He had long thick eyelashes.

The bridge of the Prophet's nose was high. His mouth was wide, and there were spaces between each of his teeth. His teeth were bright, appearing like tiny hailstones when he smiled, and they sparkled as he talked.

The Prophet's beard was black, thick and full, covering most of his chest. A few gray hair showed by his ear lobes and chin.

Head, Neck and Hair

The Prophet ﷺ had a large head on a long neck. His hair was slightly curly, and he wore it parted in the middle. Sometimes he kept his hair so long it touched both shoulders, while at other times it fell just above or below his ear lobes. He had a few gray hair above his forehead, but there were no more than twenty gray hairs on his head and beard together.

Limbs

The Prophet ﷺ was big-boned with large elbows, shoulders, knees, and wrists. His palms and feet were wide. His arms were heavy and hairy, and his heels and calves were light. He had broad hirsute shoulders, but his chest was broad and hairless, with only a line of hair running from his chest to his navel.

Build and Stature

The Prophet ﷺ was of a medium build, being neither fat nor thin. He had a straight body. Although he was not particularly tall, he rose above most men in height.

Fragrance

Several of the Prophet's Companions have mentioned a fragrance, sweeter than any perfume, emanating from the Prophet's body. Anas ﷺ said, "I never smelt any musk or any other such perfume that was as sweet as the fragrance of the Prophet ﷺ." Jâbir ﷺ said, "The Prophet's fragrance lingered after he left, and we could tell which path he had taken by sniffing the air." If the Prophet ﷺ happened to shake hands with anyone, the fragrance would remain with that person for

the whole day. When he spread his hand over a child's head, others would discern his fragrance on the child. Umm Sulaim رضى الله عنها used to collect some of the Prophet's sweat in a small bottle and would mix it with perfume.

The Prophet's Gait

The Prophet ﷺ was swift-footed and had a firm step. He would rise sharply and walk swiftly but smoothly, as if going down a slope. He would turn swiftly and gracefully.

The Prophet ﷺ never seemed to tire when he walked, and nobody could keep pace with him. Abu Hurairah ﷺ said, "I have never seen anyone who walked as quickly as the Prophet ﷺ. It looked as if the earth rolled itself up for him when he walked. We would tire ourselves out walking with him, while he would move on with ease."

Voice and Speech

The Prophet's voice was slightly loud, his speech eloquent. He looked dignified in silence and attractive while speaking. He always spoke to the point, and his words were explicit and distinct. Quite naturally, he was a powerful orator.

He was well versed in Arabic and quite familiar with the dialects and accents of every tribe. He spoke with those who

hosted him using their own accents and dialects. He mastered and was quite eloquent at both bedouin and town speech. So he had the strength and eloquence of the bedouin dialect as well as the clarity and the splendor of the aesthetic speech of town. Above all, there was the help of Allâh embodied in the revealed Verses of the Qur'ân.

Character

The Prophet ﷺ usually seemed cheerful, and he liked to smile. Even when others were rude to him, he was never harsh and rude, unlike everybody, the more he was hurt or injured, the more clement and patient he became. The more insolence and ignorance anybody exercised against him, the more enduring he became. He never raised his voice in the market place.

If faced with a choice between two options, the Prophet ﷺ would always choose the easier one, provided that it did not lead to sin. Above everything else, he avoided sinning or anything leading to the disobedience of Allâh. He never sought revenge for any offense committed against himself, but when the Honor of Allâh was at stake, he would certainly punish the offender.

His courage, his support and his power were distinguished. He was the most courageous. He witnessed awkward and

difficult times and stood fast during them. More than once brave men and daring ones fled away leaving him alone; yet he stood with full composure facing the enemy without turning his back. All brave men must have experienced fleeing once or have been driven off the battlefield at one time except the Prophet ﷺ. 'Ali ؓ said:

> "Whenever the fight grew fierce and the eyes of fighters went red, we used to turn for help to the Prophet ﷺ for support. He was always the closest to the enemy." (*Ash-Shifa,* 1:89)

Anas ؓ said:

> "One night the people of Al-Madinah felt alarmed. People went out hurriedly towards the source of the sound, but the Prophet ﷺ had already gone ahead of them. He was on the horse of Abu Talhah (!) which had no saddle over it, and a sword was slung round his neck, and said to them: 'There is nothing to be afraid of.'" (*Sahih Al-Bukhâri,* 1:407)

He was the most modest and the first one to cast his eyes down. Abu Sa'îd Al-Khudri ؓ said:

> "He was shier than a virgin in her bedroom. When he hated a thing we read it on his face." (*Sahih Al-Bukhâri,* 1:504)

He would not stare at anybody's face. He would always cast his eyes down. He looked at the ground more than he looked skywards. The most he would look at a person was a glance

at him. Everybody willingly and modestly obeyed him. He would never name a person whom he had heard ill news about which he hated. Instead he would say: “Why do certain people do such and such…”

He never rebuked his servant, nor was he ever heard saying something unkind about anyone.

Visiting the poor, the needy and entertaining them were some of his habits. If a slave invited him, he would accept the invitation. He always sat among his friends as if he was just an ordinary person. 'Aishah رضى الله عنها said that he used to repair his shoes, sew or mend his clothes and to do what ordinary men did in their houses. After all, he was a human being like others. He used to check his own clothing for wear. Milking the ewe and catering for himself were some of his normal jobs. (*Mishkât Al-Masâbih*, 2:521)

Even before his appointment as Allâh's Messenger, the Prophet ﷺ was known as *Al-Amin* (the Trustworthy). He was the keenest and the most attentive of people's trust and was very careful to pay people's due in full. The Prophet ﷺ was the most amenable and the most yielding companion, seeing him unexpectedly, one feared him and venerated him. He who had acquaintance with him, liked him. He who describes him says:

> "I have never seen such a person, neither before nor after seeing him." (*Sahih Al-Bukhâri*, 1:503)

The Prophetic Household

The Prophet ﷺ had either eleven or twelve wives, of whom nine were alive when he passed away. A short account of each of the Mothers of the believers is given below:

1. Khadeejah bint Khuwaylid رضى الله عنها

The Prophet ﷺ married her when he was twenty-five years old. She bore all the Prophet's children except Ibraheem, and was the Prophet's only wife while she lived. She died at the age of 65, in the month of Ramadan, ten years after the Prophet ﷺ began his mission, and was buried in Hajoon.

2. Saudah bint Zam`ah رضى الله عنها

She was previously married to her cousin Sakran bin Amr. The couple embraced Islam and migrated to Abyssinia. On their return to Makkah, Sakran died. The Prophet ﷺ married Saudah in the month of Shawwal, one month after Khadeejah died. She died in Shawwal, 54 A.H.

3. Aishah Siddeeqah bint Abu Bakr Siddeeq رضى الله عنها

The Prophet ﷺ married her in Shawwal, a year after marrying Saudah. Aishah رضى الله عنها was the only virgin the Prophet ﷺ married and was regarded as the best loved of all the Prophet's wives. She was the most learned female Muslim jurist in history. She passed away on Ramadan 17, 57 A.H., And was buried in Baqi.

4. Hafsah bint Umar bin Khattab رضى الله عنها

She was married to Khunays bin Hadhafah, who died from a wound incurred at the Battle of Badr. The Prophet ﷺ married her in Sah`ban, 3 A.H., after she came out of mourning. She died in Madinah in Sha`ban, 45 A.H., at the age of 60, and was buried in Baqi'.

5. Zaynab bint Khuzaymah رضى الله عنها

She was the widow of Ubaidah bin Harith ﷺ who was martyred in the Battle of Badr. According to some others she was married to Abdullah bin Jahsh ﷺ, who was martyred in the Battle of Uhud. The Prophet ﷺ married her in 4 A.H. In the Days of Ignorance, she was known as *"Ummul-Masaakeen"* (Mother of the destitute) for her compassion toward the poor. She died in Rabi` Al-Akhir, 4 A.H., eight months after her marriage to the Prophet ﷺ . The Prophet ﷺ led her funeral prayer and buried her in Baqi'.

6. Umm Salamah, or Hind bint Abu Umayyah رضى الله عنها

She was married to Abu Salamah ﷺ. She bore several children while married to him, but he died in Jamad Al-Akhir, 4 A.H. The Prophet ﷺ married her at the end of Shawwal, 4 A.H. She was a great jurist and one of the wisest women of her time. She died in 59 A.H. At the age of 84 (other sources date her death in 62 A.H.). She was buried in Baqi'.

7. Zaynab bint Jahsh bin Riqab رضى الله عنها

She was the daughter of the Prophet's aunt Umaymah bint Abdul-Muttalib. She was initially married to Zayd bin Harithah, but the couple had problems, and Zayd divorced her. Zayd had been adopted by the Prophet ﷺ, and according to ancient Arab customs, it was unlawful for a man to marry the former wife of an adopted son. Allâh ordered the Prophet ﷺ to marry Zaynab to show that this ancient Arab custom had been abolished. The marriage took place in Dhul Qa`dah, 5 A.H. (other sources date the marriage in 4 A.H.). She died in 20 A.H. at the age of 53 and was the first to die among the Prophet's surviving wives. Umar ﷺ led the funeral prayer, and she was buried in Baqi'.

8. Juwairiyah bint Al-Harith رضى الله عنها

She was brought as a prisoner from the battle of Banu Al-Mustaliq in Sha`ban, in the year 5 or 6 A.H. and was given to Thabit bin Qays. He decided to set her free in return for a certain amount. The Prophet ﷺ paid Thabit the amount he requested, freed her and married her. Having seen this, the Muslims set free one hundred families of Banu Al-Mustaliq saying that they were in-laws of the Prophet ﷺ. Thus, she proved herself a blessing for her people. She died in Rabi` Al-Awwal, 56 A.H., At the age of 65.

9. Umm Habeebah or Ramlah bint Abi Sufyan رضى الله عنها

She came to be known as "Umm Habeebah" (the mother of Habeebah) because of her daughter, Habeebah. As the daughter of the Prophet's fierce enemy, Abu Sufyan bin Harb, she made many sacrifices for her faith and migrated to Abyssinia along with her husband, Ubaidullah bin Jahsh. Ubaidullah later converted to Christianity and died, but Umm Habeebah remained steadfast in faith. When the Prophet ﷺ sent his envoy, Amr bin Umaiyah Damri, to the king of Abyssinia, he also sent a proposal to the widowed Umm Habeebah. The king married her to the Prophet ﷺ under the escort of Shurahbeel bin Hasnah. After the Prophet ﷺ returned from Khaybar, he married Umm Habeebah in Safar or Rabi` Al-Awwal, 7 A.H. She died either in 42 or 44 A.H.

10. Safiyah bint Huyaiy bin Akhtab رضى الله عنها

She was the daughter of the chieftain of the Jewish tribe of Banu Nadir and a descendant of the Prophet Haroon (Aaron) عليه السلام. She was taken captive in Khaybar and given to the Prophet ﷺ because of her status. The Prophet ﷺ asked her to accept Islam and she did so. He then set her free and married her in 7 A.H. on the eve of the conquest of Khaybar. Her death is variously dated around 36, 50 and 52 A.H. She too was buried in Baqi'.

11. Maymoonah bint Harith Hilaliyah رضى الله عنها

She was the sister of Abbas' wife, Umm Al-Fadl Lababah Al Kubra bint Harith Hilaliyah. The Prophet ﷺ married her in Dhul Qa`dah, 7 A.H. She came to the Prophet ﷺ as his bride at Sarf, nine miles outside Makkah. She also died at Sarf in 38, 61 or 62 A.H. And was buried there. Her grave site is known even today.

The Prophet ﷺ also had a maid named Mariya Qibtiya (Mary the Copt), who was presented to him by Muqauqis. She bore the Prophet ﷺ a son named Ibraheem. She died in 15 or 16 A.H. And was buried in Baqi.

What others said about Prophet Muhammad ﷺ

George Bernard Shaw said:

"He must be called the Savior of Humanity. I believe that if a man like him were to assume the dictatorship of a modern world, he would succeed in solving its problems in a way that would bring it much-needed peace and happiness."

(*The Genuine Islam*, Singapore, Vol. 1, No 8, 1936)

Lamartine, the celebrated historian says:

"If greatness of purpose, smallness of means and astounding results are the three criteria of human genius, who could dare to compare any great man in modern history with Muhammad? The most famous men created arms, laws and empires only. They founded, if anything at all, no more than material powers which often crumbled away before their eyes. This man moved not only armies, legislations, empires, peoples and dynasties, but millions of men in one-third of the then inhabited world; and more than that, he moved the

altars, The gods, the religions, the ideas, the beliefs and souls...his forbearance in victory, his ambition, which was entirely devoted to one idea and in no manner striving for an empire; his endless prayers, his mystic conversations with God, his death and his triumph over death; all these attest not to an impostor but to a firm conviction which gave him the power to restore a dogma. This dogma was twofold, the unity of God and the immateriality of God; the former telling what God is, the latter telling what God is not; the one overthrowing false gods with the sword, the other starting an idea with words.

Philosopher, orator, apostle, legislator, warrior conqueror of ideas, restorer, of rational dogmas, of a cult without images, the founder of twenty terrestrial empires and of one spiritual empire, that is MUHAMMAD. As regards all the standards by which Human Greatness may be measured, we may ask, is there any man greater than he?"

(Lamartine, *'Histoire de la Turqie, Paris'*, 1854, Vol. II, pp. 276-277)

Michael H. Hart says:

"My choice of Muhammad to lead the list of the world's most influential persons may surprise some readers and may be questioned by others, but he was the only man in history who was supremely successful on both the religious and secular levels."

(M.H. Hart, *'The 100: A Ranking of the most influential persons in history'*, New York, 1978, p.33)

Conclusion

It is impossible to adequately describe the Prophet Muhammad's character, his mission and successes, and significance for all humanity. Definitely he is on an exalted standard of character. In the previous sections, there is merely a brief account of important and influential aspects of his character.

The Prophet Muhammad ﷺ was sent by Allâh to guide the people towards the religion chosen by Allâh for them. Almost all the Prophets of Allâh have suffered much hardships for the fulfillment of the mission assigned to them. So was the case with the Prophet Muhammad ﷺ. He faced many difficulties in his efforts to call the people towards the Oneness of Allâh. His compassion, mercy and love towards other people and his determination for justice in all dealings are such qualities that should be mentioned again and again so that these may be recalled whenever the name of the Prophet ﷺ is mentioned.

I pray that Allâh bless this small work, and forgive me for falling short of my lofty goal. And I pray that Allâh bless the Prophet, his family, and his righteous Companions. May Allâh grant us a place under the Prophet's standard on the Day of Judgment. *Ameen*!